Puns

Intended

By Barbara Noel

Order this book online at www.trafford.com
or email orders@trafford.com

Most Trafford titles are also available at major online book retailers.

Note for Librarians: A cataloguing record for this book is available from Library and Archives Canada at www.collectionscanada.ca/amicus/index-e.html

Printed in Victoria, BC, Canada.

ISBN: 978-1-4269-1726-4

Our mission is to efficiently provide the world's finest, most comprehensive book publishing service, enabling every author to experience success. To find out how to publish your book, your way, and have it available worldwide, visit us online at www.trafford.com

Trafford rev. 9/29/2009

 www.trafford.com

North America & international
toll-free: 1 888 232 4444 (USA & Canada)
phone: 250 383 6864 ♦ fax: 812 355 4082

Dedicated to the residents, management, and staff of the
Grizzly Peak Retirement Home
in Missoula, Montana

Acknowledgements:

To my daughter Nancy, who kept my typewriter in working order, supplied me with paper and pens, and was a sounding board for my puns

To my granddaughter Tammy Norman, her husband Dave, and daughter Rebecca for their editorial and computer skills

To a friend Joy Nelson who steered me to Jeannie Green, provider of self-publishing material

To the residents of the Grizzly Peak Retirement Home for their enthusiasm and encouragement in the pursuit of my life-long dream of publishing a book of puns, and specifically to these managers and residents:

Lloyd and Lannie Gillan
Jim and Cindy Sellers
Fran Andersen
Maybelle Bockemeuhl
Margaret Carson
Patsy Fillenworth
Jerry Kempthorne

Jean Kimble
Mugs Pieters
Hazel Phelps
Glenna Mae Reish
Betty Schultes
Jean Sommers
Ellen Wilson

Contents

I. Animal World

Domestic Bliss

Dog Days

- Lassie's movie career went from wags to riches

- A dog's owner usually gets a welcome waggin'

- When a puppy gets stuck on a housetop he becomes a Piddler on the Roof

- You can find some dogs barking up the wrong tree

- Animal crackers are fireworks for dogs

- A lawsuit against hunting dogs is a case in point

- Rest stops for dogs are called toiletrees

- Canines should carry their own doggy bags

- Dogs can't travel by rail unless they are well-trained

- You don't want to fight a dog if he is a Boxer

- Members of the Kennel Club belong to the Pet Set

- Little dogs playing in the snow are called Slush Puppies

- You can call your dog Hamlet if he's a Great Dane

- A dog sled is a Polar Coaster
- A movie starring dogs will be a howling success
- You can always teach a bloodhound new treks

Cat Tales

- A fat cat is a flabby tabby
- A lazy cat lets his motor idle
- The feline that delivers your newspaper is a copy cat
- Give a cat a saucer of milk and he lives in the lap of luxury
- A feline x-ray is a cat scan
- Some felines become cat burglars
- Cats like to take a little nip once in awhile
- Different breeds of cats can be found in a Catalog
- Some cats have their own scratch pads

Farm Yarns

Cattle Calls

- The dairy farmer that was a football player retired his jersey
- A cattle rancher could go bankrupt if the stock market crashes
- You shouldn't milk a cow unless she's in the mood
- A happy cow can become the laughing stock of the herd

- A cattle rancher kept track of his herd on a Bulletin board

- You can inject your herd with blue dye and end up with blue chip stock

- When a cow gives birth she becomes deCalfinated

- Stagecoach drivers need to learn to hold their horses

- For cattle every day is hay day

- Livestock always ends up as dead meat

- A cattle auction becomes a stock exchange

- For a farmer a dry cow is a milk dud

- When a cow is in heat she's ready for a bull session

- If you brand cattle you could end up as a stock holder

- When you lose out at a cattle auction it's a bidder disappointment

Horse Play and Goat Fun

- When a rodeo horse goes broke he's out of bucks

- Horses can swim upstream without a saddle

- Some horse trainers are filly busters

- Stallions have their share of night mares

- Nanny Goat told Billy Goat she was not in the mood for kidding

- Breakfast food for goats is Goatmeal

- Mountain goats like to vacation at a seaside goatel

Sheep Dip and Hog Wash

- Pigs have their own porking lot
- Pork sausage is always on sale on Groundhog Day
- Sheep get their wool sheared at the baa baa shop
- When sheep get cut they bleat
- The motto of the sheepherder is: to shear and shear alike
- The black sheep of the family is a dyed-in-the-wool democrat
- Sheepherders like to keep their sheep behind flocked doors
- You can pull the wool over a sheep's eyes
- A prize pig is a squeal of fortune
- A rich hog farmer ran his own piggy bank
- The best way to haul female sheep is by ewe haul
- Pigs running on the highway are road hogs
- The stories about Ms. Piggy's laundry are hog wash
- A hamstring is a leash for potbellied pigs

Call of the Wild

Fish Stories

- Some fishermen like to go sole searching
- Swordfish settle their differences by dueling
- Mrs. Oyster was the Mother of Pearl

- Raising tropical fish is a small scale operation

- A disturbed octopus can be armed and dangerous

- Fish never engage in sports where nets are involved

- An octopus is the only sea creature that welcomes you with open arms

- A shrimp fisherman sells his catch to a prawn broker

- The beauty of a fish is only fin deep

- The newest game show at Marine World is the Whale of Fortune

- Tartar sauce is good for the sole

- The tail of a whale is a fluke

The Birds and the Bees

- The only way to cook a crazy duck is in a quack pot

- A baby chick on rollers is a cheep skate

- You should stay away from the henhouse when there is fowl language spoken

- In the year 2000 the Audobon Society celebrated the tern of the century

- The praying mantis is a church goer

- When a mosquito visits your home he's on his pest behavior

- The sign on the hen house said: May the chickens roost in peace

- Migratory birds should use their tern signals

- A talking bird is more interesting than a spelling bee
- When you cross a hawk with a horse you get horse feathers
- Birds doo it everywhere
- Ducks have webbed feet so they can go river dancing
- A fat bird is a round robin
- A crazy crow is a raven maniac
- The cheapest way to drill holes is to hire a woodpecker
- If you want your turkey stuffed go to a taxidermist
- A turquoise colored bird is an aqua duck
- For a pelican a large fish will fill the bill
- The only birds you see in Atlanta are the Falcons
- The poop deck on a cruise ship is only for the sea gulls
- A chicken might refuse to be roasted until it's fully dressed
- Abandoned poultry can be adopted by Foster Farms
- Even a good hunting guide could lead you on a wild goose chase
- Mother Nature left the pelicans with outstanding bills
- A condor's nest is a condorminium
- A bird in the hand is messy
- All pea hens get invited to cocktail parties
- Stolen eggs from the hen house are considered poached
- The ducks were the first to have a web site

- Since birds don't go to school they have to learn to wing it

- A centipede likes to put all his legs in one basket

- When a queen bee moves into a new hive it's a whole new ball of wax

- Honey is only seen in the hives of the beeholder

- Harvesting honey could lead to a sting operation

- The question of the day is "Do bees go on honeymoons?"

- You have swatter's rights when it comes to flying insects

- Bee farmers are always looking for a free bee

- For a bee there's no place like comb

- Some bees start out in bumble beginnings

- Mrs. Firefly got all dressed up but there was no place to glow

- Fireflies are glitter bugs

- Whooping cranes can be identified by their persistent coughs

- A mosquito is a skin diver

- One insect show turned out to be a Bee movie

- A cricket is a humbug

- An enterprising developer opened up a saloon for bar flies and stool pigeons

- Oysters prefer water beds

- Before going bird watching check the feather report

- One Boy Scout thought bird watching would make him an Eagle Scout
- Black forest clocks could be full of ticks
- You need to keep the flies out of the ointment

Reptiles and Rodents

- A skunk is born with the Power of Positive Stinking
- Playanimal Magazine features a skunk as its scenterfold
- Turtles have their own tax shellter
- A bashful tortoise won't come out of its shell
- When you break up a rabbit litter you split hares
- A nut-gathering squirrel has its own cache and carry operation
- The rodent's new book is called Little Mouse on the Prairie
- An intelligent snake is a smart asp
- Frogs seem to possess their own croak of genius
- Grooming rabbits is called hare styling
- Mickey and Minnie Mouse are currently starring in the Mice Capades
- Leave it to Beaver to build a dam
- A reptile show often has a snake preview
- It was a bad hare day when the tortoise won the race
- You don't tell a secret to a snake if he's a rattle tale

- A dehydrated alligator needs some gator aid
- Oregon State sports fans are eager beavers
- If you have a rich raccoon you can call him Ty
- Rabbits in Scotland like to play hopscotch
- A squirrel's nest is a Nutcracker Suite
- A snake that crawls onto a car window is a windshield viper
- Bats love a fly by night existence
- These days even the frogs have their own pads
- A blow to the head of a turtle will leave him shell-shocked

Zoo Town

- A coyote in the southwest is known as the Hound of Music
- A game hunter will do anything for a buck
- When elephants travel they carry their own trunks
- A bear den is called a cubby hole
- Zookeepers are a cagey lot
- You can get breaking gnus from Africa
- There are dandy lions at the zoo
- Tigers and zebras don't have to earn their stripes
- Siberian tigers and snow leopards are cool cats
- Veterinarians have to take the Hippocratic oath
- Hyenas are considered the laughing stock of Africa

- Fighting among apes is called gorilla warfare

- Sometimes a grizzly can be overbearing

- Writing an animal story is aardvark

- Photographing a young deer can leave you with fawned memories

- A crazy female deer is a weirdoe

- A buffalo lets the chips fall where they may

- A zoologist has to learn all the bear facts

- When you order a camel in Egypt specify one hump or two

- The jungle monkeys have their own swing-a-longs

- A checker playing kangaroo wears a jump suit

- An Australian mystic is called a kanguru

II. Body and Soul

Medical Practice

- Some bacteria are strep teasers

- The discovery of penicillin was worth its weight in mold

- Some pharmaceutical companies can be described as Houses of Pill Repute

- Some mental patients suffer from notion sickness

- A patient who didn't want cardiac surgery finally had a change of heart

- Tattoo artists do all their own needlework

- A book of podiatry contains a lot of footnotes

- Mother Nature is the creator of Designer Genes

- After a measles outbreak the Public Health Department made some rash statements

- A skull keeps you in a good frame of mind

- Donating your organs is a dead giveaway

- A patient with a sore throat should watch his strep

- When bacteria finish school they germinate

- An unshaven face is a stubble field

- Tread softly in the pharmacy so that you do not wake the sleeping pills

- Two chemists who work in the penicillin laboratory are having a budding romance and are looking forward to growing mold together

- A pillow is a good stool softener

- To apply for an optometry license you have to show your eye-school diploma

- Twins are wombmates

- When a mountain climber broke his arm it was Slingtime in the Rockies

- The doctors searched in vein for the blood clot

- In today's medical jargon a bed pan is a porta-potty

- When the Norseman needed a heart transplant he only wanted a Swedeheart

- Pimples are foreign lesions

- Cosmetic surgery is done in the line of beauty

- A medical clinic in coal country only performs miner surgery

- The only people that get breaks are the orthopedic surgeons

- Companions for the deaf are called hearing aides

- To the dermatologist belong the boils

- Salvation Army Santa's are afflicted with jingle fever

- A sign over the maternity ward reads: To Heir is Human
- A clone is a cell mate
- Dentures are held together with tooth paste
- When you vote at an optometrist convention the eyes have it
- A tooth fairy is a gay dentist
- If your tooth is loose you know the Yanks are coming
- A trip to the doctor often means you have to grin and bare it
- Orthopedic doctors find it hard to cast a shadow
- Women consider their breasts as treasure chests
- Don't get hypnotized in winter because you might be in for a cold spell
- You can't think if you lose your mind
- A couple of drug addicts promised to stay together until Meth did them part
- Cosmetic surgery is a Nip and Tuck procedure
- You could make headlines if you don't stop frowning
- It's your legs that make you an upstanding citizen
- When a woman reaches menopause she joins the Over the Pill gang
- You can always trace the roots of people with dyed hair
- Glasses are For Your Eyes Only

- You can always change surgeons if you don't like the way they operate

- A convicted doctor showed up in court wearing his malpractice suit

- A training film for surgeons is called A Scar is Born

- An eye clinic is a site for sore eyes

- The psychologists named their practice Headquarters

- A marriage counselor is a psycho built for two

- A hypnotist is a tranceformer

- To get rid of an itch you have to start from scratch

- When a urologist asked his patient what she did all day she said she just piddled around

- Some people don't see eye to eye because their nose gets in the way

- A nightly injection is a shot in the dark

Oh What a Belief It Is

- People go to church for a faith lifting

- A pastor is the soul support of his church

- If you cross a cherry with an apple, you get a chapel

- For church employees every day is pray day

- In a funeral home every shroud has a silver lining

- A church shredding machine is a holy tearer

- Some churches believe in prophet sharing

- For a church attendee scrubbing the mission means cleaning the kitchen

- When a church needs a new organ, check the donor list

- Only church candles give out holy smoke

- When you attend a wake it's usually a beautiful mourning

- Church attendees believe they get just what they prayed for

- Jesus was chosen the Person of the Weak

- Nuns are creatures of habit

- When God told his people to go forth and multiply he never dreamed someone would invent the calculator

- When selecting a new minister the congregation chose the one with the best offering

- When a flood threatened to destroy a church the minister asked the Lord to forgive him for the damning he was about to do

- A decision to become a nun is called Planned Sisterhood

- A good sermon is fueled by soular energy

- All religious sects should respect the rites of others

- When a church has two pastors one must become the Prime Minister

III. Brands of Humor

Buy-Products

- Burma Shave signs along the highway were considered smile posts

- If you own a Mustang you can Ford every stream

- If you drop your slow cooker it could become a crackpot

- At a recent paper convention many tissues were discussed

- Fabric dying at home used to be a Ritual

- Role Aids are used to help actors remember their lines

- It is no Secret that some deodorants are Banned in Boston

- Some wine growers are Grape Nuts

- A man who reads his newspaper at breakfast is behind the Times

- Some people think that the Stanley Steamer is a vegetable cooker

- You don't have to take the Pledge of allegiance before dusting furniture

- For a good wrap session call Reynolds

- A salad dressing company is part owner of the Mayo clinic

- Without gas a painter can't make his Van Gogh

- They call a five cent beer Nickelob

- A microScope is a small bottle of mouthwash

- If you have dirty dishes at night you can wait until Dawn to wash them

- Mr. Shortening was considered the Count of Monte Crisco

- For a food parade A & W built a root beer float

- If you want a good relationship with an insurance company it should be Mutual

- Spain will never have an oil shortage because they will always have Oil of Ole'

- A city bank is a good place for a Stick-Up

- You can trace genealogy back to Levi Strauss

- Your guests will applaud you for putting on Ritz

- If your paper towels are missing you can hire a Bounty hunter

- A saloon in Alaska is known as the Klondike Bar

- A poor economy might mean closing the Gap

- It's hard to change a tire without a Cracker Jack

- Hallmark is a good cardware store

- The Lipton company is proud of their experTeas

- Granny Smith is a member of the Apple Corps

Window Shopping

- One fast food restaurant has an arch rival in St. Louis

- One cereal claims their product is made of hole grain

- At a seaside grocery store you can only buy soap when the Tide is in

- There's a new garden tool in Hawaii called Don Hoe

- Smucker's has a lot of jam sessions

- Recliners are made for Lazy Boys

- To run a successful business you need to trend lightly and carry a big stock

- Oscar Meyer is a real wiener

- A track coach tells his team to run like Deere

- A new book on billiards is full of Q-tips

- The assistant musical director was a Band Aide

- When the coach of a football team sweats he could send in a Right Guard

- When Johnny was late at a concert you were short of Cash

- Johnny Cash could have named his daughter Petty

- Hostilities among cast members could lead to Star Wars

- The Texas Ranger's double is called the Clone Ranger

- A gold colored scarf is a Midas muffler

- Robbing an armored truck could end in the Brink of disaster

- An army sergeant headquartered in Alaska soon became a Kool Aide

- Sean Connery made his millions in the Bond market

- Sean Connery, Roger Moore, Pierce Brosnan, and Daniel Craig shared a common Bond

- The Three Musketeers rode down the Milky Way to the Mars Bar to get a Big Hunk

- In the bovine world a cow can become a Dairy Queen

- One detective agency was named: The Friendly Spies of United

- Graham is the best safecracker in town

- The Kellogg company hired a detective to find the cereal killer

- Donald was arrested on Trumped-up charges

- One golf course has a Bunker named Archie

IV. Crime and Punishment

Fuzz Budgets

- A group of lawyers got together and opened a plea market

- The testimony in the cosmetic case turned out to be made-up

- The trial of the illegal immigrant turned out to be a borderline case

- Many criminals are eligible for the Crook of the Month club

- A snitch in time could save a crime

- A drug agent was called Narco Polo

- There isn't a cue in the case of the missing pool table

- No lawyer likes to try a basket case

- A detective makes a good snooper man

- A good fingerprint leaves a lasting impression

- Lawyers who travel by air rest their cases in the overhead bin

- When you track a criminal at twilight it is called a five-o'clock shadow

- One lawyer called his apartment a legal pad

- The Nome lawyer specialized in cold cases

- Some policemen have arresting personalities

- Some police patrol the beaches when they have a crime wave

- If you catch Sherlock Holmes sleeping he's probably working on a pillow case

- It will be a short trial if a lawyer brings his brief case to court

- Every day police turn over a new thief

- A witness described a murder suspect as dressed to kill

- With an increase in the grime rate more cleaning agents are needed

- Putting a plaster cast on a prisoner could make him a hardened criminal

- A bank holdup in March is known as the first robbin' of spring

- A juvenile motorcycle gang was called the Little Red Riding Hoods

- A murder suspect sat on the hot seat when he was grilled

- One criminal was caught stealing toothpaste and selling it on the plaque market

- A country boy was convinced to join a bunch of hoodlums because he was farmed and dangerous

- The suspect who stole gold jewelry pleaded not gilty

- Shoplifters possess the gift of grab

- The son of a Wisconsin butcher was the wurst brat in town

- The unknown deceased millionaire was listed as John Dough

- Prisoners often become good pen pals

- Stolen jewelry is often here today and pawned tomorrow

- A con man is a super duper

- One prisoner wrote a book on the Art of Crooking

- A Catholic criminal gave himself up for Lent

Dice and Vice

Gambling fever

- Las Vegas cops are still looking for the one-armed bandit

- Wheeling and Dealing means Roulette and Black Jack

- A sign on a Casino says: Your Buck Stops Here

- Playing the slot machine all day makes you an all-day sucker

- At the poker table a Royal Flush is The Deal of Fortune

- When you play roulette you are spinning your wheels

- You shouldn't gamble on meat products because the steaks are too high

- When a crap shooter loses his turn at the table it's pair a dice lost
- New Chinese gamblers are called Fortune Rookies
- Slot machines are cash guzzlers
- The swat team identified the killer bee by its yellow jacket
- A casino is where a fool and his money are soon parted
- Shooting craps is a matter of shake, rattle, and roll
- Hopeful poker players stand around waiting for the changing of the cards
- A casino can be hazardous to your wealth
- Old crap shooters never die they just fade away

Vice

- Dealing with heroin means you're a horse trader
- Marijuana plants need a good potting soil
- Pot parties in Hawaii are held in grass shacks
- When the grass is greener on the other side marijuana must be growing
- For a drug addict marijuana is the pot at the end of the rainbow
- Good advice for drug pushers is to keep within the speed limit
- Smoking marijuana is a joint venture
- Some dinner parties turn out to be potluck

- Many heroin users pack their own bags before going on a trip

- Stealing a sleeping child is kidnapping

- Arsonists like to disobey orders to cease fire

V. Domestic Scenes

Love and Marriage

The Mating Game

- If you marry a man with a penthouse you will get a groom with a view

- In the olden days when a lady dropped her handkerchief it led to some hanky panky

- When the freshness goes out of a marriage it could be caused by a stale mate

- When ordering a groom don't get stuck with junk male

- If a boyfriend gives you goosebumps it's better than charging for them

- Family stories are based on the theory of Relativity

- A sign over the marriage bureau said: Pay Now, Play Later

- When you marry a poet you take him for better or verse

- People who get married twice must have an altar ego

- An unemployed husband may be on wife support

The Children's Hour

- To be a boy scout leader one has to learn all the ropes

- A royal baby delivered in flight is considered heirborne

- When an expectant mother is ready to deliver she must grin and bear it

- When boys grown up they soon become broad-minded

- Babies are like the weather there's always a change coming

- A kindergarten teacher gave her class a block party

- Today's kids like to buy shoes with no strings attached

- A baby sucks its thumb because it's finger-lickin' good

- Kid who love french fries are tater tots

- A child who is afraid of Santa Claus suffers from Claustrophobia

- A father told his teenage son not to swear before the ladies, let them swear first

- Pregnancy is the time from here to maternity

- When a student gets a zero on a test all his studying is for naught

- An aunt always brought her nephew a sack of pennies; she was his Penny Ante

- Young men consider life just a matter of fun and dames

- One couple named their son Filbert because he was such a nut

- One mother gets her daughter up after the son rises

- The population explosion is a birthquake

Senior Citizens

- Old age is the age when happy hour is a long nap
- Becoming a senior citizen is something you don't have to apply for, it comes with the territory
- A grandfather clock is an old timer
- Retirement is classified as Maturity Leave
- Snowbirds like to go south for the winter since almost everyday is Sunday
- Seniors are never too old to yearn
- Most seniors live to a gripe old age
- My grandfather had a wooden leg and my grandmother had a cedar chest
- The aging process is called slipping beauty
- An aunt that is over 100 years old is an auntique
- It's better to be looking down at the grass than being under it
- If your grandfather swears too much take him to a Cursing Home
- Senior citizens look forward to their reclining years
- Middle-aged spread is the waist of time
- Senior citizens like to live in the past lane

- You will feel more comfortable among strangers if you carry your social security card

House Coping

Food For Thought

- The latest apple cider news is hot off the press
- You can't get eggs from an eggplant
- A hamburger is a cheap steak
- A pastry chef can always bring home the bakin'
- A grandmother's cereal is called Granflakes
- After a butcher shop robbery the police came up with the missing links
- A reporter got the scoop of the day from an ice cream parlor
- Natural bread is made with wild flours
- The story about pretzel-making has a happy bending
- Crazy looking pickles are called daffydills
- Filing a mining claim in the Alps is a Swiss stake
- Some Deli workers can't cut the mustard
- An incompetent baker gets his just desserts
- A chocolate lover is a cocoanut
- A seafood restaurant is a home for battered fish
- Grapes are pressed for time

- Ordering more than one drink at the bar makes you a second glass citizen

- After a night on the town nobody can read between the wines

- If your wife tells you to go for a Wok don't come home with a Crock Pot

- Kitchen helpers are pan handlers

- A sign on a saloon said: Keep a glow profile

- There are a few ground rules for making coffee

- A bread maker knows how to raise dough when it is kneaded

- When you throw up a pumpkin it comes down squash

- Eating cherries makes for a lot of pit stops

- At a candy factory a sucker is born every minute

- Crushed ice is just chips off the old block

- When you are out of dough you are out of bread

- Salads are made for all seasonings

- Nut-filled cookies are Nutcracker Sweets

- Blackberries are red when they're green

- Growing herbs is thyme consuming

- A martial arts instructor went to a butcher shop and came out with a karate chop

- Running an apple orchard makes you subject to the windfall profits tax

- If the steaks are too high bet on the hamburger
- It's best to harvest cranberries before they get bogged down
- Some cookies are held together with ginger snaps
- When you make taffy you have to pull together
- Guys that like chips and cheese are Nacho men
- A review of the newest lunar restaurant said: the food is great but it has no atmosphere
- More people eat finger food than tofud

Neighborhood Bar

- A beer truck driver doesn't handle well when loaded
- The beer drinkers theme song is: Keg of My Heart
- The last drink in the bar is called the parting shot
- Some drinking buddies often beat you to the punch
- Drinking before dinner means wetting your appetite
- There is always some beer pressure among breweries
- Most drivers of liquor trucks come in loaded
- When an alcoholic comedian gets rehabilitated he comes back to the stage as a cured ham
- Some beer drinkers are on their last kegs
- Harbor Lites is a beer sold on the waterfront
- Drinking in the shower is apt to dampen your spirits
- Expensive champagne is in a glass all by itself

- A convicted bartender had to spend the rest of his life behind bars

- The best moonshine is made in the still of the night

- When you order wine on a cruise not any old port will do

- Exceptional wine is made on the Planet of the Grapes

- Jumping over a bottle of whiskey is called hopscotch

- The Moby Dick cocktail packs a whale of a kick

- An alcoholic stands on the drink of disaster

- You can get a good glass of beer at the malt shop

- When a party guest passes out he joins the urban sprawl

- A keg of beer can be a barrel of fun

- Mountain climbers take their alcohol with them so they can have Scotch on the rocks

- At a self-service bar you can call your own shots

- When both sides of the street have bars they are double-jointed

Weigh of Life

- Dieters do a lot of weight lifting

- Overeating makes the world go round

- Dieters who fail tend to leave it all behind

- Some people will go to the edge of the girth to lose weight

- A starvation diet gives you very few binge benefits

- Some appetizers are made for skinny dipping

- Most dieters don't lean hard enough

- The weak shall inherit the girth

- For a successful diet plan consult the Weighs and Means committee

- Overeating can lead to something big

- For some people dieting is just a weigh of life

- Losing weight depends upon your power of positive shrinking

- Gravity is responsible for a belly flop

- Dieting makes you get rid of the Incredible Bulk

- If you don't diet, there will be a plumpy road ahead

- Sometimes dieting is a losing battle

- Diet food is considered slim pickins'

- A compulsive eater has a lot to show for it

- An obese dinner companion could be a stuffed shirt

- To watch your weight just look in the mirror

- Skinny people have nothing to lose and everything to gain

- Dieting can best be described as breaking the pound barrier

Fashion Lines

- A necktie is string around the collar

- Fitting rooms in a department store are clothes quarters

- A bra is just a booby trap

- Hot pants are considered thermal underwear

- The best place to purchase neckwear is Thailand

- Western footwear can only be sold at a Bootique

- When a wealthy woman buys a fur coat it is usually on the fur of the moment

- Linings for coats can be downloaded

- If you don't want to buy a tuxedo suit yourself

- You can put on a happy face with make-up

- A glove is a handbag

- Writing about blankets makes a good cover story

- After a men's underwear sale, boxers seem to be in short supply

- A model's life is full of wine and poses

- For wrinkled garments never underestimate the power of the press

- A bikini protects the property but doesn't obstruct the view

- If you are wearing a hair piece during a windstorm you could blow your top

- Making buttons could be a fastenating job

- You need earmuffs for lobal warming

- If you need softwear buy a cashmere sweater

- If you wear long underwear keep your trap shut

- Shoes are sold by the foot

- A sleeping bag is a napsack

- Dresses are used for slip covers

Household Hints

- The new housekeeper was a sweeping beauty

- A carpet salesman is a rug pusher

- A remodeled basement could get you on the best cellar's list

- The highlight of a dining room is the chandelier

- If you want a custom-made carpet leave it to weaver

- You can purchase pedal pushers on the Isle of Capri

- There are many products for cleaning stained glass windows

- A furnace makes a good housewarming present

- You need to call a housekeeper for broom service

- When your ceiling is too low you can always raise the roof

- You can't tell a mattress by its cover

- A knitted afghan has a lot of fringe benefits

VI. The Entertainers

Artistic talent

Paint Chips

- A color coordinator uses all the pigments of his imagination
- Painters never draw straws
- A country landscape is a rural mural
- Some artists work their way through collage
- Some artists take brush-up courses to improve their technique
- Some artists don't paint ocean views unless the coast is clear
- Most artists like to draw their own conclusions
- You can see a picture show at an art gallery
- One New York painter left his art in San Francisco
- A fire in a picture gallery could lead to a lot of art burn
- Great paintings are made by strokes of genius
- An artist can draw a crowd while painting a landscape

Dancing Feet

- One burlesque show features Stars and Strips forever

- A ballet dancer develops by leaps and bounds

- Harem girls like to dance sheik to sheik

- Girls in a chorus line get a kick out of dancing

- There is a new hip joint in town called The Slipped Disco

Musical Notes

- A strip tease musical is called My Bare Lady

- Not all musical composers are noteworthy

- Only bagpipe music is recorded on Scotch Tape

- Some composers write music just for the record

- Russian ballet is called Dancing with the Czars

- In a Texas orchestra the trombone is known as a long horn

- You have to pull a lot of strings to play a harp

- A successful disc jockey needs to be radioactive

- Competition among the brass section could lead to the Battle of the Saxes

- A rock group called the Boomerangs has made a comeback

- The Firecrackers are an explosive rock band

- When a soprano's voice cracks there's trouble on the high Cs

- Most violinists like to fiddle around

- No drummers like to beat around the bush
- Recording music on discs was a groovy idea
- Students in music like to end their days on a high note
- A good guitar player is Lord of the Strings
- In a string quartet there's always room for cello
- A good percussionist can drum up business
- A part-time musical director is a semi-conductor
- Musically inclined geologists are rock hounds

Poetic Justice

- These days a poet must be diverseified
- Poets often get together to talk over old rhymes
- Writing a book is a novel way to start a career
- There's no point to the story of the broken pencil
- Interviews with publishers are hard to get because so many are already overbooked
- A book about two comedians is called the Tale of Two Witties
- You can add cornstarch to a mystery story to thicken the plot
- To make a long story short cut off its tale
- A book that contains three different mystery stories is a Thrillogy

- A Christmas mystery story is about Gold, Frankincense, and Myrrder

- A successful writer looks at the world thru prose-colored glasses

Stage Struck

- A puppeteer can always pull strings

- Tightrope walkers are high-strung people

- A good comedian possesses True Wit

- When Lady Guinevere had a date with Sir Lancelot it was a knight to remember

- Movie studios own a lot of reel property

- Comedians from Rio de Janeiro are called Brazil nuts

- In Sherwood forest the outhouse was called Little John

- A Shakespearean cocktail is served As You Like It

- A horror movie has a lot of cringe benefits

- A young comedian is a quipper snapper

- If you're a ventriloquist two heads are better than one

- The proceeds from the box office are just play money

VII. Foreign Affairs

Americana

Continental

- People like California despite its faults

- In plains country you learn to live off the flat of the land

- It was May 18, 1980 when Mt. St. Helens blew her top and made quite an ash of herself

- The Lord of the Onion Rings resides in Walla Walla

- Potters in the southwest like to make clay while the sun shines

- One Polish fisherman told his friend he was out of line

- Square dancing is a petticoat function

- The vigilantes were known for their hanging parties

- The scenery along the Oregon coast is shore pretty

- The birth of our nation was not accomplished without a few labor pains

- Terrorists upset the Big Apple cart

- New England barbers are called Yankee Clippers

39

- Florida sponsors the March of Limes

- When the nude parachutist jumped out over Florida it was Moon Over Miami

- The Grand Canyon is more than just a pretty face

North to Alaska

- One young Eskimo ran away from Nome

- Lack of sleep at the North Pole could leave you with Arctic circles

- Alaskan citizens deposit their money in Fairbanks

- Igloo is what keeps Eskimo homes together

- The Alaskan deli specializes in cold cuts

- When the Alaskan gold rush was over all the butchers pulled up their steaks

- An unusually hot summer almost Baked Alaska

Aloha Traditions

- A Hawaiian computer expert is a nerd of paradise

- Many Hawaiian girls go to luaus with their poi friends

- The reason Pearl Harbor was bombed is because she drank too many Mai Tais

- The biggest women's movement in Hawaii is the hula

- Hawaiians went into the sugar business because they liked to raise cane

- Striking sugar plantation workers were called the Cane Mutiny

Abroadminded

Europe

- An Australian hiker trekked through the desert and ended up with Aborigi knees

- When a Russian student graduates from college he is known as a Leningrad

- The amnesiac from Prague was a blank Czech

- A royal coronation could be postponed on account of reign

- Englishmen never get tired of the Knight life

- Too much French wine will get you plastered in Paris

- The fall of the roman umpire came after being hit by a fast ball

- A secret romance in Scotland is known as a clandestine affair

- Courting a Scotch lass could lead to a Highland Fling

- Adventure stories about Ireland are written in Wild Irish Prose

- In England a second class apartment is known as a B flat

- Ireland is the place to go for Dublin your money

- Green lollipops are made for the Lick of the Irish

- Horseback riders in Warsaw are interviewed by a Gallup Poll

- The Scots are famous for their ice cream scones

- To remove caviar from a Siberian fish you need to call a Russian sturgeon

- For an Italian there's no place like Rome

- If you want to watch the London news, turn to the English Channel

- When you go out with a Hollander you go Dutch treat

- A married couple in Czechoslovakia are called Czechmates

- Napoleon should always order a whole chicken so he can pull a Bonaparte

- You can make a French toast with a glass of wine

- You can get a great view of Paris from the eyeful tower

- It takes a long time to develop a new perfume because aroma wasn't built in a day

- When you talk about English mothers mums the word

- A guillotine executioner gets his orders from headquarters

- When Sir Galahad gets caught in a windstorm he becomes a knightingale

- Before an Englishman is knighted he has to pay a sir charge

The Orient

- Rich Japanese are called millyenaires

- When you travel to the Far East it's hard to get oriented

- Disappointed geisha girls are called misfortune cookies

- Japanese parents have a lot of Rising Sons

- You need a good character study to learn the Chinese alphabet

- A Chinese astronaut took a wok on the moon

- A Chinese chef was fired from his job because he was caught sleep Woking

- A boat store in China is run by a junk dealer

Mid-East

- The Star of Bethlehem is the light before Christmas

- You call an Arabian dairy farmer a Milk Sheik

- Crossing the Sahara Desert is long time no sea

- Arabian pies are served Allah mode

- An Egyptian course in Mummification requires a few wrap sessions

- African love potions are known as Afrodisiacs

- African politics are influenced by propUganda

- In Iraq you can see bag ladies and Baghdads

- An Egyptian college fraternity is called Chi Rho

- The only suitable flooring for an African hut is Congoleum

- Indian war planes never open their Bombay doors

VIII.   Group Dynamics

Armed Forces

- A small navy woman is a microWave

- Sailors are given latrine duty by the Chief Potty officer

- Navy communication officers make good anchor men

- Any holes on deck are filled by the Putty officer

- Wearing a windbreaker is one way to avoid the draft

- After a hitch in the navy sailors remember all of the fleeting moments

- Each army supply depot has its own powder room

- A marine who doesn't live up to corps standards is a submarine

- At a Texas military post a sergeant sent his platoon out to drill for oil

- The Coast Guard maintains its own Coast office

- Army WACs are always wishing for male call

- Barbecuing aboard ship is called offshore grilling

- Navy women are called Liberty belles

- Stories about navy women are old Waves tales

- An army dentist became a drill sergeant

Ghost Stories

- When you toast a ghost you lift your spirits

- Before witches go out for Halloween they have to file a fright plan

- At the next séance you could be the ghost of honor

- For a ghost to live in a high-class neighborhood he needs to do some house haunting

- Haunted ships are under investigation by the ghost guard

- Ghosts never charge for haunting houses because they are free spirits

- On Halloween you can send your friendly ghost a booquet of flowers

- You shouldn't enter a haunted house unless the ghost is clear

- An ocean beach is home to sandwitches

- A ghost has no visible means of support

- A ghost says boo because that's his only way of spooking

- At a Halloween party you never know which witch is witch

- At a recent séance the medium couldn't get her trancemission to work

- Breakfast for a spirit is ghost toasties

Happy Wanderers

- Hoboes are compulsive ramblers
- When you're a hobo every day is a bummer
- Hoboes exercise on trampolines
- Pan handlers are summer bummers
- A patched coat is a bum wrap
- A chef is often called a pan handler

In the Buff

- When a nudist asks you for a date, tell him you have nothing to wear
- A nudist gambler could be on a winning streak
- Some people can't bare to join a nudist colony
- A female nudist bought a blanket so she could be a Cover Girl
- A nude runner is a streak of nature
- There is hardware and software, but the nudists have no wear

People at Large

- Santa is the Claus that refreshes
- A tired Santa Claus makes for a Cross Kringle
- Santa keeps his clothes in the Clauset

- The petroleum engineer believes that oils well that ends well

- Computer operators make good mousekeepers

- Sanitary engineers are always down in the dumps

- An arsonist is a flame thrower

- Some balding men still enjoy the fringe benefits

- One chief got brave reviews for his hunting ability

- An Indian mother sent her son to the store for some TP and he came back with a Wigwam

- Seamstresses have their work cut out for them

- Hiring a funny seamstress could keep you in stitches

- One cannibal suffered from indigestion because he ate all the people who disagreed with him

- The son of a cannibal chief was expelled from school because he tried to butter up the teacher

- You need an electrician to light up your life

- Travel agents like to put the best route forward

- A tobacco chewer has to make a lot of spit stops

- A tobacco chewing father has a son who is his spitting image

- A Hindi will walk on nails just to prove a point

- Firefighters belong in the Hall of Flame

- A strip tease artist was called Tangerine because she had a license to peel

- When Eve told Adam she wanted some new clothes he told her just turn over a new leaf

- Cobblers are the sole supporters of their families

- An archeologist's career lies in ruins

- A Cuban space walker is a Castronaut

- Demolition experts had a blast at their last convention

- The Flying Nun got her start in a pilot episode

- Mr. Spock was a Trek Star

- Drinking buddies are coffee mates

- A gentleman who invites a lady out for a cocktail is liquid dating

- People who live in stone houses shouldn't throw glasses

- The meteorologist that spoke at a weather conference was a cloud pleaser

- The number of haircutters in America was determined by a Barber Poll

- You can go to a beautician for comb improvement

- Road construction workers go to a dentist to complete their bridgework

- Telephone operators have their own hang-ups

- Candy factory workers like to take their toffee breaks

- At a victory party, some prize fighters will serve the knockout punch

- During the frontier days many passengers had stage fright

- Some fountain employees are soda jerks

- After lunch carpenters return to the sawing board

- Manicurists like to keep their tools in a nail box

- Watchmakers need a vacation to unwind

- At a watchmaker's convention you can have the time of your life

- You shouldn't date an architect because he always changes his plans

- When you see a bathing beauty at the seashore it's worth wading for

- Office workers should know the fax of life

- Some students take an accounting course because they believe there is safety in numbers

- A carpet installer is a floorist

- Garbage collectors went on strike when they found out that grime doesn't pay

IX. Holocost Of Living

Money Matters

The Buck Stops Here

- You're rich if you have money left over at the end of the month

- Couples that smoke dope together can file a joint income tax return

- A centimeter is a parking meter that only takes pennies

- Money is the loot of all evil

- When your frozen assets start to thaw you'll have a nice slush fund

- Liquid assets are those you hide in your water bed

- Hot money could burn a hole in your pocket

- It takes a lot of money to live in a free country

- You need a lot of money to enjoy wine, women, and song

- These days you have to learn to make it on your loan

- There's always a dirty old man among the filthy rich

- The slogan of a coin collector is: Let the good dimes roll

- You have to start with good sense to make dollars

- You can get more fiber from an Apple than a Blackberry

- It takes a lot of cash to carry out your dreams

- The world rotates on its taxes

- Country assessors are known as Millage People

- The Great Divide is when the government separates you from your money

- No matter how you slice it Uncle Sam gets his share of the bread

- A credit card is a buy pass

Marketing Quips

- Investing in adhesives could lead to a stuck market

- The members of the ironing board held a press conference

- One furniture store went bankrupt when they invested in rocking shares

- A lot of investors would like a slice of the Blackberry pie

- You can use your hedge funds to protect your property

- A flea market is no place to take your dog

- A good stockbroker can give you a clean bill of wealth

- Counterfeiters are good at passing the buck

- A new book on money is called For Whom the Bill Tolls

- Automobile tires sell at inflated prices

- When the bank employee opens up the wrong safety deposit box its not your vault

- It's bad when you lose your balance especially at a bank

- The IRS agent always has a tax to grind

- When you get your tire fixed they charge a flat fee

- A good investor likes to have his fingers in every buy

- Lumber mill employees are required to attend all the board meetings

- Contract negotiations with cranberry farmers often get bogged down

- Commodity brokers get together to talk over gold times

Monkey Business

Mismanagement

- Shop windows are designed for innocent buy-standers

- One glassmaking company almost went broke

- The cost of fireworks has skyrocketed

- A slogan for a lumber mill is: We ply harder

- A gum factory in Tennessee is called the Chattanooga Chew Chew

- A new roofing company in town just hung up their shingle

- Buying perfume is just a matter of exchanging dollars for scents

- When William Sr. and William Jr. send out their store statements they expect their customers to pay their Bills promptly

Shop Talk

- If you work for a quarry breaking up is hard to do

- Before you buy your next mattress you should sleep on it

- When a new business opened the sign said: A Store is Born

- Business will bloom if you open a flower shop

- The Indian food is great at the New Delhi

- Window shoppers are eyebrowsing

- A business card for a cattle rancher read: Leave the Driving to Us

- At a ski resort business is always going downhill

- Making buttons could be a fastenating profession

- A change for the better was provided by disposable diapers

- Holding a business meeting in a sauna could lead to some heated discussions

- Deluxe garbage trucks only take the pick of the litter

- When a nursery is out of merchandise it is caught with its plants down

- A brassiere company believes that it's what's up front that counts

- Florists are petal pushers

- Breweries are under a lot of beer pressure

- Coal miners are learning to take their lumps

- Show and sell is the motto of the Real Estate business

- Successful realtors need to do a good deed every day

- Most herbologists have thyme on their hands

- In a sweater factory the workers are close knit

- Cowboys in Texas borrow money from the Loan Ranger

- A dishonest counter top installer is a counterfitter

- Some ironworkers get a license to steel

- Most watchmakers travel by plane so they can see how time flies

- When you attend a coal miners party you should be sootably dressed

- To cover a nudist camp store the newspaper sent out a free-glance photographer

- A mattress tester was paid for lying down on the job

- One sink business went down the drain

- Ditch diggers wear trench coats

- You should see a realtor if you have a lot on your mind

- The sale of rifles was so successful it was worth repeating

- The president of a yardstick maker was an exalted ruler while his wife was a meter maid

- One car parts store had a bumper crop

- A slogan of one electricians' union was: Many Hands Make Light Work

- An automotive union is always open for carbitration

- The first day on a new job could be Trial and Terror

- Garment workers belong in the Piece Corps

- Some computer operators go home at night with a chip on their shoulder

- Employees on a coffee plantation are called grounds keepers

- Some workers at a cleaning company are called Bleach Boys

- Bus boys are called Dish Jockeys

- Some barber shops are a cut above the rest

- When you are self-employed you've got to learn to mind your own business

- When the farmer needed to fix his fence he called Western Union to send him a wire

- A depressed peanut market is called The Peanut Butter Crunch

- The middle class is halfway between the debt set and the jet set

- Some millionaires keep their cache in a Swiss Bank

- You can study geology at the School of Hard Rocks

- When a farmer harvests his crop it's hay day

- An expensive English apartment could keep you flat broke

- For a farmer low prices seem to go against the grain

- You can find a lot of crude men in the oil business

X. Politicking

Government

- The best way to win an election is to stay ahead of the front runner

- The voting booth is the mark-it place for an election

- It's necessary to get your overseas shots if you want diplomatic immunity

- The government might even make hitchhikers pay a thumb tax

- Offering gifts to government officials could lead to bribal warfare

- Congressional meetings are sometimes referred to as Sit Coms

- Congress has its own soft soap to brainwash the people

- The only difference between Congress and the people is that congress passes the bills and the people pay them

- The new dance step in government is the cabinet shuffle

- The favorite refreshment in Congress is Federal Ade

- Congress is not foolproof

- The American people are like sheep and the government is out to fleece them

- There is no power shortage in the country; the politicians have it all

- Some politicians come up with premises they can't keep

XI. All Sorts Of Sports

Team Spirit

Kick, Run, and Pass

- When a new athlete fails to make the team, that's the way the rookie crumbles

- Football players can be penalized 15 yards for quipping

- The Heisman trophy winner slept with his window open so he could be #1 in the draft

- Changing of the guard means a football substitute

- A poor place kicker was caught with his punts down

- A football team that plays in the Big Apple could have a few turnovers

- All Canadian football players belong to the 'eh' team

- Most quarterbacks have passing thoughts

- The Green Bay football team always plays to a packed house

- The Philadelphia football team shaved their heads so they could be the bald Eagles

- All the best coaches are in the stands

On Base

- There could be slide effects from stealing bases

- When a baseball player was told to bundt he said that will be a piece of cake

- A good outfielder can become Lord of the Flies

- A good baseball player has swatter's rights

- The players of a baseball team walked out when the umpire called a strike

- Houston baseball fans are Astronuts

Solo Flights

Hole-in-One

- An amateur golfer was arrested for driving without a license

- One golfer always wore two pairs of socks in case he got a hole-in-one

- The golfing green is a sight to be holed

- Golfer dads teach their kids how to drive

- Some golfers play better when they are below par

- A golfer played very poorly in the South African tournament but he was lucky because he found a diamond in the rough

- Good golf greens are for the birdies

- In golf there are different strokes for different folks

- Some golfers are haunted by the bogey man

- After a golf lesson the instructor took his students out for a test drive

- The annual country club dance is the golf ball

- English golfers are never late for tee time

- In golf lingo the 19th hole is bar for the course

Courting Disaster and Boxer Rebellion

- The women's Hawaiian basketball team is called the Hula Hoops

- For a basketball player it's a tall, tall world after all

- You'll have a heavy date with a Sumo wrestler

- If you like to throw your weight around try Judo

- The sign on a boxer's locker said: Out to Punch

- They named the street behind the boxing ring Muhammad Ali

- When prize fighters go on strike it is a Boxer Rebellion

Clearing the Waterfront

- If one fishing lure doesn't work get a rebait

- When you buy a rowboat you're back in the paddle again

- A coxswain of a racing shell is King of the Rowed

- Shuffleboard is always played on a marked deck

- Climbing a mountain can be a breathtaking experience

- To be a good figure skater you need to do more than one good turn a day

- Some mountain climbing students never make the grade

- The rent for a skydiving plane is high, but the fall is free

Assorted Sports

- An archer was informed about the arrow of his ways

- An avid jogger is a road runner

- Jogging on your vacation means you are running away from home

- The manager of a roller rink is a cheap skate

- When a hockey player scores a goal it's a stroke of puck

- All the costs of scuba diving are classified as depth charges

- You need a pair o' chutes to go tandem diving

- Hunters meet together in the fall to shoot the bull

- Learning to shoot a gun requires a course in trigggernometry

XII. Travel-Log

Locomotion

Motor Pools

- You buy a motor home to get away from it all and then you take it all with you

- Motorists should look before they beep

- When you are not driving your fancy car be sure to turn off the Porsche light

- Trees hauled by trucks make good travelogs

- Calling the interstate a freeway is ludicrous when we all have to pay for it

- A magician can make his car disappear when he turns it into a garage

- The story of Henry Ford and the model T is covered in his autobiography

- It takes a lot of highjacking to change a truck tire

- Speeding on the turnpike takes its toll

- A lot of camping rigs are trailer made

- A sign on an antique car reads: May You Rust In Peace

- Many race car drivers are under crews control
- At a camping rally you can't see the forest for the RV's
- Purchasing a motor home is an investment in wheel estate
- Some motorists like to play the passing game
- When driving his runaway truck the driver asked the Lord to give him a brake

Plane Talk

- Flight attendants are just plane people
- The sign on the airport tarmac read: Landing Room Only
- Flight training is a form of higher education
- If you are afraid to fly just express yourself
- The red-eye flight from New York to the Pacific coast could leave you sleepless in Seattle
- The cost of a helicopter ride includes the hover charge

Ship Ahoy

- Pier pressure is used to keep down the berth rate
- A sailing ship is called mast transit
- When a single girl takes a cruise it could be her last maiden voyage
- Noah's boat was designed by an arkitech
- It's hard to pilot a ship in dire straits

- A shipment of snails from France was labeled SS Cargot

- The captain of a ship is in charge of crews control

XIII. Unclassyfied Information

Lines of Our Times

- Railroads have good track records

- A little diamond is a baby carat

- Diamond cutters are good at slicing carats

- A small town farmacy can fill all your animal medications

- With an increase in the grime rate more cleaning agents are needed

- A coffee cup can be personalized with a mug shot

- Accumulating excess land makes you a ground hog

- Gravity will cause you to be grounded

- People who don't have a hobby are craft dodgers

- When radials wear out they should be retired

- If you put a 20 foot cord on a telephone you can talk longer

- If your words are loaded don't pull the trigger

- Don't feed the fake animals because they are already overstuffed

- The story of the big mountain is all a bluff

- A beautiful sunset is a cloud pleaser

- Some rocks are boulder than others

- Sunshine is responsible for global warming and moonshine causes a drinking problem

- In a dense forest old trees die with their roots on

- Rainfall could make flood water too big for their ditches

- Icy pavement is called Skid Row

- The monkey on a man's back could be a tattoo

- A vacation is time off for good behavior

- A young tree needs a lot of room to set down roots

- Hypnotism is called rapid transcendence

- When a sign on the road shows dangerous curves ahead it doesn't mean a bevy of pretty girls

- There is no shock absorber made for an earthquake

- Dad used a popsicle to cut the grain

- The inventor of the paper clip must have had a twisted mind

- A sarcastic telegram is a barbed wire

- A palm tree is sad when it loses its best fronds

- Knick-knacks have a long shelf life

- Junk is something you throw away two weeks before you need it

- You can now mail a package with no strings attached

- A Christmas drinking song is: Roll Out the Carols

- The sign on a nuclear plant read: Gone Fission

- Humpty Dumpty was an egg head

- If you tell a lie you could be punished by the truth fairy

- An old palm tree can sometimes be out of dates

- To express your opinion send it parcel post

- Swearing seems to be a universal Cusstom

- Private tutoring means you're in a class by yourself

- Roses become best buds before blossoming

- A new lawn mower will give you better grass mileage

- You have to stay awake if you want to beat the nods

- Without a shower you could become the scum of the earth

- Mother Nature depends on gravity to keep people grounded

- If you invest in real estate you get a lot for your money

- You can find the powder room next to the ammunition dump

- Venus de Milo must have been part of the disarmament treaty

- Paper bags have no sacks life

- If you are living on borrowed time, you shouldn't wear someone else's watch

- An artificial tree is considered a fake fir

- A weed is a plant with nine lives

- If you are invited to a shower, be sure to bring an umbrella
- It takes two cacti to make a prickly pair
- An alarm clock gets ticked off once in a while
- Thinking takes a lot of skull practice
- A line is a circle that has gone straight
- A new post office got the stamp of approval
- After you plant your flowers you can throw in the trowel
- Getting hung for a crime you didn't commit is a pain in the neck
- It takes a lot of reeding to weave a basket
- Every piece of coal is a carbon copy of itself
- When the wind gets too violent you can always shoot the breeze
- Hurricane storms are Rains of Terror
- An icicle can keep a stiff upper drip
- A sad tree is a weeping willow
- Sometimes a blue sky can become overclouded
- Environmental pollution can be eliminated by using earth control pills
- A drizzle is a drop going steady
- If you want brilliant flowers plant flash bulbs
- If you don't want your family tree exposed don't dig up the roots

- You can get lip service at a county fair booth

- Billboard advertising is a form of sign language

- You can build bridges over troubled waters

- Winter leaves you with memories of the way we BRRRRRRRR

- Long lines of people are called wait watchers

- Maintaining a cemetery plot could present a grave problem

- An old spinning wheel becomes an heirloom

- A tour though a perfume factory is a scentimental journey

- A man pulled up his carpet so he could see the floor show

- A hand mixer can make you stir crazy

- Buried treasure becomes sleeping booty

- Long lines at the Post Office could lead to a stampede

- The sign on the frontier town sheriff's office read: Out to Lynch

- People who snore always fall asleep first

- Ocean waves returned to the sea after taking shore leave

- A new hot dog franchise was called Mustards' Last Stand

- A car heater is partly responsible for mobile warming

- The noise from New year's Eve fireworks goes in one year and out the other

- A sex change is a gender bender

- On an old-fashioned wall telephone you could make crank calls

- Circling the globe is considered a whirlwind tour

- Life if good. It would be hard to live without it